Ten-Second Tongue Twisters

Mike Artell

Illustrated by
Buck Jones

STERLING

New York / London
www.sterlingpublishing.com/kids

Library of Congress Cataloging-in-Publication Data
Artell, Mike.
    Ten-second tongue twisters / Mike Artell ; illustrated by Buck Jones.
        p. cm.
    Includes index.
    ISBN 1-4027-2258-3
    1. Tongue twisters. I. Title: 10 second tongue twisters. II. Jones, Buck.
III. Title.

PN6371.5.A767 2006
398.8—dc22

                                                                    2005023459

Lot #:
10 9 8 7 6 5 4 3 2 1
09/10
Published by Sterling Publishing Co., Inc.
387 Park Avenue South, New York, NY 10016

Distributed in Canada by Sterling Publishing
c/o Canadian Manda Group, 165 Dufferin Street
Toronto, Ontario, Canada M6K 3H6
Distributed in Australia by Capricorn Link (Australia) Pty. Ltd.
P.O. Box 704, Windsor, NSW 2756, Australia

Sterling ISBN 978-1-4027-7858-2

For information about custom editions, special sales, premium and
corporate purchases, please contact Sterling Special Sales
Department at 800-805-5489 or specialsales@sterlingpublishing.com.

Contents

Introduction

How many times can you say each of these tongue twisters in ten seconds?

They're easy to say just once or twice. They become difficult only when you try to say them as many times as you can in just ten seconds. The classic example of a tongue twister that's easy to say fast once, but almost impossible to say fast more than five times is "toy boat." The faster you say it, the more likely it is that you will say "toy boyt." Most of these tongue twisters are like that—easy to say once, twice, or even three times, but very difficult to say many times, especially when you add the pressure of a ten-second clock.

Do you have a clock ready? If so, see how many times you can say these tongue twisters in ten seconds.

Family Picnic

Flapjack Snack

Jack stacked the flapjack snack in the kayak.
Jack stacked the flapjack snack in the kayak.
Jack stacked the flapjack snack in the kayak.

The Cello Man

The fellow with the cello ate marshmallow Jell-O.
The fellow with the cello ate marshmallow Jell-O.
The fellow with the cello ate marshmallow Jell-O.

Mosquito Mashing Michelle

Michelle mashed mosquitoes, making a messy mosquito mush.
Michelle mashed mosquitoes, making a messy mosquito mush.
Michelle mashed mosquitoes, making a messy mosquito mush.

Gesundheit!

Steve sneezed on his sleeve.
Steve sneezed on his sleeve.
Steve sneezed on his sleeve.

B-z-z-z

The bugs buzzed and bugged Buzz.
The bugs buzzed and bugged Buzz.
The bugs buzzed and bugged Buzz.

Plates, Please!

Please pass the plastic plates.
Please pass the plastic plates.
Please pass the plastic plates.

Stop, Chip!

Stop sticking the chopsticks in the chips, Chip.
Stop sticking the chopsticks in the chips, Chip.
Stop sticking the chopsticks in the chips, Chip.

Wet Weather or Not

Would you rather wet weather or would you rather
   weather that wasn't wet?
Would you rather wet weather or would you rather
   weather that wasn't wet?

Crab Claws

Claude cracks crab claws.
Claude cracks crab claws.
Claude cracks crab claws.

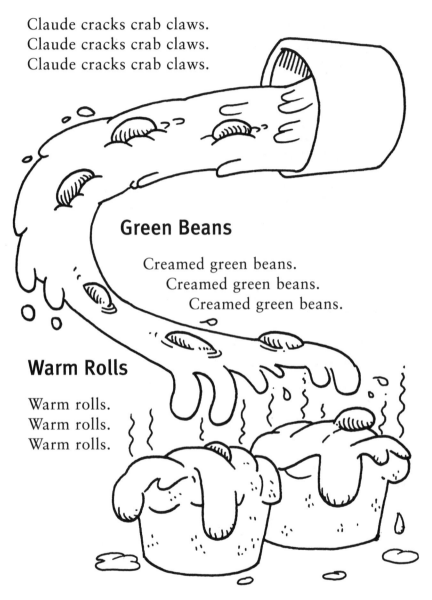

Green Beans

Creamed green beans.
Creamed green beans.
Creamed green beans.

Warm Rolls

Warm rolls.
Warm rolls.
Warm rolls.

Hickock Hiccupped

Henry Hickock hiccupped.
Henry Hickock hiccupped.
Henry Hickock hiccupped.

Pop 'n' Pup

Papa petted Pepper's puppy.
Papa petted Pepper's puppy.
Papa petted Pepper's puppy.

Troy Tried

Troy tried tying two tires together.
Troy tried tying two tires together.
Troy tried tying two tires together.

Calm Colin

Colin calmly combed the calico cat.
Colin calmly combed the calico cat.
Colin calmly combed the calico cat.

Disappearing Pears

A pair of pears apparently disappeared after Peter appeared near the place where the pears were placed.
A pair of pears apparently disappeared after Peter appeared near the place where the pears were placed.

Greg's Grown!

Grandma gasped at Greg's growth.
Grandma gasped at Greg's growth.
Grandma gasped at Greg's growth.

Ice Cream

Extreme ice cream.
Extreme ice cream.
Extreme ice cream.

Toffee Toppings

Tasty toffee toppings.
Tasty toffee toppings.
Tasty toffee toppings.

My Sore Thumb

I have a sore thumb. A thorn stuck my thumb and
  made my thumb sore.
I have a sore thumb. A thorn stuck my thumb and
  made my thumb sore.

Mark's Muddy Mounds

Mark made many muddy mounds.
  Mark made many muddy mounds.
    Mark made many muddy mounds.

Short Shorts

Hippos Hiccup

Hippos hiccup.
Hippos hiccup.
Hippos hiccup.

Truck Trunks

Truck trunks.
Truck trunks.
Truck trunks.

Cheek-to-Cheek

Cheek-to-cheek.
Cheek-to-cheek.
Cheek-to-cheek.

Gross Ghosts

Gross ghosts.
Gross ghosts.
Gross ghosts.

The Lazies

Lazy little ladies.
Lazy little ladies.
Lazy little ladies.

Cracked Corks

Cracked corks.
Cracked corks.
Cracked corks.

Luscious Licorice

Luscious lip-licking
   licorice.
Luscious lip-licking
   licorice.
Luscious lip-licking
   licorice.

Wheel Rims

Rear wheel rims.
Rear wheel rims.
Rear wheel rims.

Red Wagon

Wide red wagon.
  Wide red wagon.
    Wide red wagon.

Slippery Slopes

Slippery, sloppy ski slopes.
Slippery, sloppy ski slopes.
Slippery, sloppy ski slopes.

Fritters

Fresh flounder fritters.
Fresh flounder fritters.
Fresh flounder fritters.

Creamy Creamer

Creamy coffee creamer.
Creamy coffee creamer.
Creamy coffee creamer.

Flimsy Foil

Flat flimsy foil.
Flat flimsy foil.
Flat flimsy foil.

Rings and Rings

Wet, round rings.
Wet, round rings.
Wet, round rings.

3 **Working World**

Why Wes Went West

One reason why Wes went West was to work as a
  wrestler.
One reason why Wes went West was to work as a
  wrestler.
One reason why Wes went West was to work as a
  wrestler.

Cliff-Climbin' Kip

Kip was a cliff climber. Kip climbed cliffs.
Kip was a cliff climber. Kip climbed cliffs.
Kip was a cliff climber. Kip climbed cliffs.

Cuckoo Clock Cleaner

Cooper cleaned cuckoo clocks.
Cooper cleaned cuckoo clocks.
Cooper cleaned cuckoo clocks.

Hurricane Hunter Hunter

Hunter is a hurricane hunter. Hunter hunts hurricanes.
Hunter is a hurricane hunter. Hunter hunts hurricanes.
Hunter is a hurricane hunter. Hunter hunts hurricanes.

Kirk's Work

Kirk drained dirty ditches during the day.
Kirk drained dirty ditches during the day.
Kirk drained dirty ditches during the day.

Purple Peanuts

Peter planted purple peanut plants in his peanut
  patch. The peanut plants Peter planted produced
  purple peanuts. Peter politely packed the peanuts
  for people who purchased the popular purple
  produce.

Soleful Stu

Stu sold shoe soles by the shoe store.
Stu sold shoe soles by the shoe store.
Stu sold shoe soles by the shoe store.

Two Taco Tasters

The two taco tasters took turns tasting tacos.
The two taco tasters took turns tasting tacos.
The two taco tasters took turns tasting tacos.

Little Yodeler

The little yodeler learned to yodel loudly.
The little yodeler learned to yodel loudly.
The little yodeler learned to yodel loudly.

Pit Picker Paul

Paul picked pits from prunes. Paul was a pro at
picking prune pits.
Paul picked pits from prunes. Paul was a pro at
picking prune pits.
Paul picked pits from prunes. Paul was a pro at
picking prune pits.

Wright Writes Wrong

William Wright was a writer. Wright had a right to
write, but Wright's writings were rarely right. What
Wright wrote was wrong. What was wrong with
what Wright wrote was Wright's weak words.

Tarantula Training

Tanya trains tarantulas in a tiny Texas town. Training tarantulas is a tricky task. Tanya trains two tarantulas at a time.

French Bread Bakers

French bread bakers bake fresh French bread.
French bread bakers bake fresh French bread.
French bread bakers bake fresh French bread.

Street Sweepers

Street sweepers sweep streets.
Street sweepers sweep streets.
Street sweepers sweep streets.

Rice Rap

Wayne went to work as a rice wrapper. He wrapped
white rice really well.
Wayne went to work as a rice wrapper. He wrapped
white rice really well.
Wayne went to work as a rice wrapper. He wrapped
white rice really well.

Percy the Pickle Picker

Percy was a pickle picker. He picked pickles perfectly
and was promoted to pickle packer. Percy packed
pickles proudly He proved that pickle pickers can
pack pickles properly.

Paolo Plowed the Pasture

Paolo plowed the pasture prior to planting peanuts.
Paolo plowed the pasture prior to planting peanuts.
Paolo plowed the pasture prior to planting peanuts.

Sal's Superb Sailing Skill

Sal was so skilled at sailing that some sailors stood
still to see Sal sail.
Sal was so skilled at sailing that some sailors stood
still to see Sal sail.
Sal was so skilled at sailing that some sailors stood
still to see Sal sail.

Porter the Sports Reporter

Porter is a sports reporter. He purports to support sports, but his sports reports are poor.
Porter is a sports reporter. He purports to support sports, but his sports reports are poor.

Mango Man

That man grows mangoes by the mangroves.
That man grows mangoes by the mangroves.
That man grows mangoes by the mangroves.

Cuttin' Carpet

A couple of carpet cutters carefully cut the cream-colored carpet.
A couple of carpet cutters carefully cut the cream-colored carpet.
A couple of carpet cutters carefully cut the cream-colored carpet.

Road Workers Rode

The road workers rode to work on the road.
The road workers rode to work on the road.
The road workers rode to work on the road.

4

Vacation Situation

Shore Story

Shirley is sure the shore on the north shore is shorter
  than the shore on the south shore.
Shirley is sure the shore on the north shore is shorter
  than the shore on the south shore.
Shirley is sure the shore on the north shore is shorter
  than the shore on the south shore.

Steve Skied

Steve skied and skinned his knees.
Steve skied and skinned his knees.
Steve skied and skinned his knees.

Oh, Blair!

Blair wore a bad pair of plaid pants.
Blair wore a bad pair of plaid pants.
Blair wore a bad pair of plaid pants.

Lester's Lost Loafers

Lester lost his leather loafers.
Lester lost his leather loafers.
Lester lost his leather loafers.

Larry, Linda, Landon, and London

Larry likes London. Linda likes London less. Landon
    likes London least.
Larry likes London. Linda likes London less. Landon
    likes London least.
Larry likes London. Linda likes London less. Landon
    likes London least.

Gate Guard Garb

The gate guard wore guard garb.
The gate guard wore guard garb.
The gate guard wore guard garb.

Tall Ship's Sails Installed

The sailors started installing the tall ship's sails.
The sailors started installing the tall ship's sails.
The sailors started installing the tall ship's sails.

Left Raft Right Raft

Is the left life raft the right life raft, or is the right life
raft the right life raft?
Is the left life raft the right life raft, or is the right life
raft the right life raft?
Is the left life raft the right life raft, or is the right life
raft the right life raft?

Black Backpacks

The backpacks on our backs are black backpacks.
The backpacks on our backs are black backpacks.
The backpacks on our backs are black backpacks.

Savannah in Havana

Savannah ate a banana in a cabana in Havana.
Savannah ate a banana in a cabana in Havana.
Savannah ate a banana in a cabana in Havana.

Train Tickets to Tucson

Tori traded Taylor train tickets to Tucson for ten tacos.
Tori traded Taylor train tickets to Tucson for ten tacos.
Tori traded Taylor train tickets to Tucson for ten tacos.

Tori Tickled

Tori tickled the tired ticket-taker.
Tori tickled the tired ticket-taker.
Tori tickled the tired ticket-taker.

Big-bellied Bellboys

Both big-bellied bellboys belched boldly.
Both big-bellied bellboys belched boldly.
Both big-bellied bellboys belched boldly.

Bridgette's Brother Built a Bridge

Bridgitte's brother built a brick bridge by the
boulders beneath the bluffs.
Bridgitte's brother built a brick bridge by the
boulders beneath the bluffs.
Bridgitte's brother built a brick bridge by the
boulders beneath the bluffs.

Wet Winter Weather

Wet winter weather with wicked wet winds.
Wet winter weather with wicked wet winds.
Wet winter weather with wicked wet winds.

Touring Turkey

Two tired tourists took turns touring Turkey.
Two tired tourists took turns touring Turkey.
Two tired tourists took turns touring Turkey.

Where Oh Where?

Where are you? Are you where you were, or are you
where you are?
Where are you? Are you where you were, or are you
where you are?
Where are you? Are you where you were, or are you
where you are?

Sherman Shops

Sherman shops for shirts at the shirt shop and for
shorts at the shorts shop.
Sherman shops for shirts at the shirt shop and for
shorts at the shorts shop.
Sherman shops for shirts at the shirt shop and for
shorts at the shorts shop.

Slippers Shoppers

Several shoppers stopped to shop for slippers.
Several shoppers stopped to shop for slippers.
Several shoppers stopped to shop for slippers.

Jane's and Shane's Change

Jane, is your change the same as Shane's change?
Jane, is your change the same as Shane's change?
Jane, is your change the same as Shane's change?

What Scarlett Saw

Scarlett saw some Scottish soccer stars.
Scarlett saw some Scottish soccer stars.
Scarlett saw some Scottish soccer stars.

Throne Stone Shone

We were shown the stone that shone on the throne.
We were shown the stone that shone on the throne.
We were shown the stone that shone on the throne.

5

Let Me Count the Ways

Four Foolish Florists

Four foolish florists flew to Florida.
Four foolish florists flew to Florida.
Four foolish florists flew to Florida.

Freddy Found Five

Freddy found five fried fish.
Freddy found five fried fish.
Freddy found five fried fish.

Stella's Cell Phone Fell

Stella's cell phone fell seven floors down steel stairs.
Stella's cell phone fell seven floors down steel stairs.
Stella's cell phone fell seven floors down steel stairs.

What Sherry Did

Sherry sanded seven shelves.
Sherry sanded seven shelves.
Sherry sanded seven shelves.

Howard's Hounds

How many hounds does Howard have? Howard has a
hundred hounds that help Howard hunt.
How many hounds does Howard have? Howard has a
hundred hounds that help Howard hunt.

Two Tortoises

Two tortoises took turns tossing toasted tortillas.
Two tortoises took turns tossing toasted tortillas.
Two tortoises took turns tossing toasted tortillas.

Nine Gnats Gnawed Knees

Nine gnats gnawed Norm's knees.
Nine gnats gnawed Norm's knees.
Nine gnats gnawed Norm's knees.

Five Fat Flies

Five fat flies flew fast.
Five fat flies flew fast.
Five fat flies flew fast.

Four Furry Feet

Four furry feet full of fat fleas.
Four furry feet full of fat fleas.
Four furry feet full of fat fleas.

What Wombats Won't

One wombat won't walk and one wombat won't run.
One wombat won't walk and one wombat won't run.
One wombat won't walk and one wombat won't run.

Six Strong Safes

Six strong safes.
Six strong safes.
Six strong safes.

Allie and the Alligators

Allie entered an elevator with eleven alligators.
Allie entered an elevator with eleven alligators.
Allie entered an elevator with eleven alligators.

Two Torn Tutus

Sue took the two torn tutus to the tutu tailor and told
the tailor to sew the tutus today.
Sue took the two torn tutus to the tutu tailor and told
the tailor to sew the tutus today.

Señor Simon Saw

Señor Simon saw six stray steers sitting still.
Señor Simon saw six stray steers sitting still.
Señor Simon saw six stray steers sitting still.

Fifty-four Firefighters

Fifty-four firefighters fitfully fought the fire.
Fifty-four firefighters fitfully fought the fire.
Fifty-four firefighters fitfully fought the fire.

Sisters Suit Suitors

The two sisters the suitors saw certainly suited the suitors.
The two sisters the suitors saw certainly suited the suitors.
The two sisters the suitors saw certainly suited the suitors.

Five Friendly Frogs

Five friendly flat-footed frogs fed on fat flies.
Five friendly flat-footed frogs fed on fat flies.
Five friendly flat-footed frogs fed on fat flies.

Austin's Awesome Oysters

Austin ate out and ordered eight oysters. It was odd for Austin to order oysters, although all eight oysters Austin ordered were awesome.

6
My Amigos and Me (What's ?)

Carrie and Harry

Carrie carried Harry's hairy canary.
Carrie carried Harry's hairy canary.
Carrie carried Harry's hairy canary.

Faithful Phil

Fred's friend Phil faithfully flew the flag.
Fred's friend Phil faithfully flew the flag.
Fred's friend Phil faithfully flew the flag.

What Cara Can and Clara Can't

Cara can clean clams, but Clara can't cook clams.
Cara can clean clams, but Clara can't cook clams.
Cara can clean clams, but Clara can't cook clams.

Clara Clapped

Clara clapped when Cora cut the coconut.
Clara clapped when Cora cut the coconut.
Clara clapped when Cora cut the coconut.

Drake's Drapes

Danielle didn't drip-dry Drake's drapes.
Danielle didn't drip-dry Drake's drapes.
Danielle didn't drip-dry Drake's drapes.

Tickle Time

Tim tickled Tammy's toes Tuesday. Tammy tickled
Tim's toes Thursday.
Tim tickled Tammy's toes Tuesday. Tammy tickled
Tim's toes Thursday.

Phillip Flipped

Phillip flipped flapjacks. Phillip's fancy flapjack
flipping fascinated Phillip's friends.
Phillip flipped flapjacks. Phillip's fancy flapjack
flipping fascinated Phillip's friends.

Pete's Plain Plans

Pete's plans are plain because plain plans please Pete.
Pete's plans are plain because plain plans please Pete.
Pete's plans are plain because plain plans please Pete.

Is Justin a Jester?

Chester just suggested that Justin is just a jester.
Chester just suggested that Justin is just a jester.
Chester just suggested that Justin is just a jester.

No Nanny Aunt Annie

Nancy's Aunt Annie isn't a nanny.
Nancy's Aunt Annie isn't a nanny.
Nancy's Aunt Annie isn't a nanny.

About Chad, Chelsea, and Chuck

Chad sold the cheap cherry chair to Chelsea, who
sold the chunky Chinese chest to Chuck.
Chad sold the cheap cherry chair to Chelsea, who
sold the chunky Chinese chest to Chuck.
Chad sold the cheap cherry chair to Chelsea, who
sold the chunky Chinese chest to Chuck.

Andy's Only Anchor

Andy owns the only iron anchor on the island and
  that angers Anders.
Andy owns the only iron anchor on the island and
  that angers Anders.
Andy owns the only iron anchor on the island and
  that angers Anders.

Thanks, Shad

Shad let Sid store his sled in his sled shed.
Shad let Sid store his sled in his sled shed.
Shad let Sid store his sled in his sled shed.

Thin and Thinner

Tim's thin but Tim's twin is twice as thin as Tim.
Tim's thin but Tim's twin is twice as thin as Tim.
Tim's thin but Tim's twin is twice as thin as Tim.

Wanda's Wigs

Wanda Riggs wears weird wigs.
Wanda Riggs wears weird wigs.
Wanda Riggs wears weird wigs.

Reed Writes Well

Reed writes well and Will reads what Reed writes.
Reed writes well and Will reads what Reed writes.
Reed writes well and Will reads what Reed writes.

Reese's Racer

Grace greased Reese's green racer.
Grace greased Reese's green racer.
Grace greased Reese's green racer.

7
Twister Triplets

Thick-trunked Thistle Trees

Thistle trees have thick trunks. See these three trees
  with thick trunks? These three trees are thistle trees.
Thistle trees have thick trunks. See these three trees
  with thick trunks? These three trees are thistle trees.

Fresh Flowers

Fresh flowers. Fresher flowers. Freshest flowers.
Fresh flowers. Fresher flowers. Freshest flowers.
Fresh flowers. Fresher flowers. Freshest flowers.

Fresh Fried Fish Fillets

Fresh fried fish fillets. Fresher fried fish fillets.
  Freshest fried fish fillets.
Fresh fried fish fillets. Fresher fried fish fillets.
  Freshest fried fish fillets.
Fresh fried fish fillets. Fresher fried fish fillets.
  Freshest fried fish fillets.

Otto's Otter's Odd Odor

Otto's otter had an odd odor. It was not an ordinary
otter odor. It was an odd odor even for an otter.
Otto's otter had an odd odor. It was not an ordinary
otter odor. It was an odd odor even for an otter.

Harry Had Headaches

Harry had headaches. His hat hurt his head. "Help!"
Harry howled.
Harry had headaches. His hat hurt his head. "Help!"
Harry howled.

Wendell Went to Rent a Winch

Wednesday, Wendell went to rent a winch. Wendy'd
already rented the winch Wendell wanted to rent.
"Why did Wendy rent the winch?" Wendell
wondered.

Skin

Seal skin. Shark skin. Sheep skin.
Seal skin. Shark skin. Sheep skin.
Seal skin. Shark skin. Sheep skin.

Ostrich Nostrils

Ostrich nostrils. Ostrich nostrils. Ostrich nostrils.
Ostrich nostrils. Ostrich nostrils. Ostrich nostrils.
Ostrich nostrils. Ostrich nostrils. Ostrich nostrils.

Big Bigger Biggest

Big branch. Bigger branch. Biggest branch.
Big branch. Bigger branch. Biggest branch.
Big branch. Bigger branch. Biggest branch.

Fred Frowned

Fred frowned. Frank frowned. Phil frowned.
Fred frowned. Frank frowned. Phil frowned.
Fred frowned. Frank frowned. Phil frowned.

A Pair of Pants

A pair of pants. A pair of plaid pants. A pair of
  purple plaid pants.
A pair of pants. A pair of plaid pants. A pair of
  purple plaid pants.
A pair of pants. A pair of plaid pants. A pair of
  purple plaid pants.

8

Funny Farm

Proud Papa

A proud, proper porpoise papa.
A proud, proper porpoise papa.
A proud, proper porpoise papa.

Proper Porcupine Petting

Please pet your porcupine properly.
Please pet your porcupine properly.
Please pet your porcupine properly.

Creepy Crawly Crocs

Creepy crawly crocs crunched crispy crunchy cracker crumbs.
Creepy crawly crocs crunched crispy crunchy cracker crumbs.
Creepy crawly crocs crunched crispy crunchy cracker crumbs.

Cool Cobras

Cool cobras calmly cook chocolate.
Cool cobras calmly cook chocolate.
Cool cobras calmly cook chocolate.

Scarecrow Scares Crows

The scarecrow scares crows.
The scarecrow scares crows.
The scarecrow scares crows.

Is Howard a Coward?

"I will cower if I hear an owl howl," Howard vowed.
"I will cower if I hear an owl howl," Howard vowed.
"I will cower if I hear an owl howl," Howard vowed.

Falcons' Feathers

Falcons' feathers flap fast.
Falcons' feathers flap fast.
Falcons' feathers flap fast.

Slippery Clamshells

Slippery clamshells slowly slam shut.
Slippery clamshells slowly slam shut.
Slippery clamshells slowly slam shut.

Cat's Claws Clipped

Kate clipped the cat's claws.
Kate clipped the cat's claws.
Kate clipped the cat's claws.

Sheep Sleep

Several somber sheep slept silently.
Several somber sheep slept silently.
Several somber sheep slept silently.

Goose on the Loose!

Whose goose is loose? Is it Lou's goose or Sue's goose?
Whose goose is loose? Is it Lou's goose or Sue's goose?
Whose goose is loose? Is it Lou's goose or Sue's goose?

Elves Help Elk

The elves helped the ill elk.
The elves helped the ill elk.
The elves helped the ill elk.

Luke's Lazy Lizard

Luke's lizard looks lazy. That's a lazy lizard, Luke.
Luke's lizard looks lazy. That's a lazy lizard, Luke.
Luke's lizard looks lazy. That's a lazy lizard, Luke.

Elder Helps Hilda

Hilda held the halter as an elder helped her hold her horse.
Hilda held the halter as an elder helped her hold her horse.
Hilda held the halter as an elder helped her hold her horse.

Chubby Chimps

Chubby chimps chase shrimps.
Chubby chimps chase shrimps.
Chubby chimps chase shrimps.

Proud Peacocks

Proud peacocks playfully pecked platypuses.
Proud peacocks playfully pecked platypuses.
Proud peacocks playfully pecked platypuses.

Pig in a Patch

Put the fat pig by the fig patch.
Put the fat pig by the fig patch.
Put the fat pig by the fig patch.

Steve Snickered

Steve snickered as several sick, sneezy
snails sailed south.
    Steve snickered as several sick, sneezy
snails sailed south.
        Steve snickered as several sick,
sneezy snails sailed south.

Half-foot Heifer

I have a heifer with half a foot. Have you a half-foot
  heifer?
I have a heifer with half a foot. Have you a half-foot
  heifer?
I have a heifer with half a foot. Have you a half-foot
  heifer?

Three-toed Tree Toad

A tree toad with three toes is a three-toed tree toad.
A tree toad with three toes is a three-toed tree toad.
A tree toad with three toes is a three-toed tree toad.

Loud Bloodhound Howling

How loud does a bloodhound howl when a
  bloodhound howls out loud?
How loud does a bloodhound howl when a
  bloodhound howls out loud?
How loud does a bloodhound howl when a
  bloodhound howls out loud?

9

Basically Bad Behavior

Bad Brats

The bad brats broke the bats.
The bad brats broke the bats.
The bad brats broke the bats.

Puppy's Paws Poke Puzzle

The puppy poked its paws through the paper picture puzzle.
The puppy poked its paws through the paper picture puzzle.
The puppy poked its paws through the paper picture puzzle.

It's Bad to Brag

It's bad to brag, but Brad brags.
It's bad to brag, but Brad brags.
It's bad to brag, but Brad brags.

What Crooks Couldn't Catch

The crooks couldn't catch the caravan of caramel-colored camels carrying cargo.
The crooks couldn't catch the caravan of caramel-colored camels carrying cargo.

Sara Saw a Stegosaurus Stealing

Sara saw a stegosaurus stealing saws. "Stop!" Sara shouted. "Say you're sorry." "Sorry," the shy stegosaurus sighed.

Sly

Sly was shy, but when he spied the pigs in the pigsty,
he plotted to pilfer the pigs on the sly. But the pigs
were too sly for Sly. They slipped and slid in the
slop until Sly decided to try another sty.

My Stinky Pinkie Twinkie

You put your stinky pinkie in my Twinkie! Now it's a
stinky pinkie Twinkie.
You put your stinky pinkie in my Twinkie! Now it's a
stinky pinkie Twinkie.
You put your stinky pinkie in my Twinkie! Now it's a
stinky pinkie Twinkie.

City Kitty

A kitty in the city bit a kiddie—what a pity!
A kitty in the city bit a kiddie—what a pity!
A kitty in the city bit a kiddie—what a pity!

Dusty Dump Trucks

Two dusty dump trucks just dumped dirt at the
  junction.
Two dusty dump trucks just dumped dirt at the
  junction.
Two dusty dump trucks just dumped dirt at the
  junction.

Tracking Crushed Cracker Crumbs

Chris tracked the crushed cracker crumbs to a truck
of crackers.
Chris tracked the crushed cracker crumbs to a truck
of crackers.
Chris tracked the crushed cracker crumbs to a truck
of crackers.

Must He Munch?

Must he munch the mushy mints?
Must he munch the mushy mints?
Must he munch the mushy mints?

Brad the Braggart

Brad bragged about the bag of bones. It was a big
bag of bones (a big bag of broken bones). It's bad to
brag about a big bag of broken bones.

Peter's Prank

Peter put pickled pimiento in the puff pastry.
Peter put pickled pimiento in the puff pastry.
Peter put pickled pimiento in the puff pastry.

Ungenerous Jerry

Jerry doesn't share his cherry jelly.
Jerry doesn't share his cherry jelly.
Jerry doesn't share his cherry jelly.

Woodrow Robbed Rowan

Woodrow robbed Rowan while Rowan
was whittling wood.
Woodrow robbed Rowan while
Rowan was whittling wood.
Woodrow robbed Rowan while
Rowan was whittling wood.

Ruth's Uncouth Youths

Ruth's youths are uncouth youths—it's the truth.
Ruth's youths are uncouth youths—it's the truth.
Ruth's youths are uncouth youths—it's the truth.

Fake Facts and Factual Facts

Witches' Wishes

Witches wish weird wishes.
Witches wish weird wishes.
Witches wish weird wishes.

Silky Soft Socks

Silk socks stay silky soft.
Silk socks stay silky soft.
Silk socks stay silky soft.

She-mu He-mu

Emma's emu is a "she-mu," not a "he-mu."
Emma's emu is a "she-mu," not a "he-mu."
Emma's emu is a "she-mu," not a "he-mu."

Smelly Cellars

Smelly cellars smell stale.
Smelly cellars smell stale.
Smelly cellars smell stale.

Sticker Stuff

The thicker stickers seem to stick quicker than the
thinner stickers.
The thicker stickers seem to stick quicker than the
thinner stickers.
The thicker stickers seem to stick quicker than the
thinner stickers.

Blue Boots in Blue Box

The blue boots belong in the blue boot box.
The blue boots belong in the blue boot box.
The blue boots belong in the blue boot box.

What Every Egret Eats

Every egret eats insects—even evil egrets.
Every egret eats insects—even evil egrets.
Every egret eats insects—even evil egrets.

Clowns' Crowns

Clever clowns wear crystal crowns.
Clever clowns wear crystal crowns.
Clever clowns wear crystal crowns.

Cool Cola Cans

Keeping cola cans in a cooler keeps the cola cans cool.
    Keeping cola cans in a cooler keeps the cola cans cool.
        Keeping cola cans in a cooler keeps the cola cans cool.

Polite Police

Polite police please people.
Polite police please people.
Polite police please people.

Pretty Presents

Pretty pendants make pretty party presents.
Pretty pendants make pretty party presents.
Pretty pendants make pretty party presents.

Spitball Protocol

Students shouldn't shoot spitballs.
Students shouldn't shoot spitballs.
Students shouldn't shoot spitballs.

Prince's Parchment Paper Preference

The prince preferred parchment paper for printing
  proclamations.
The prince preferred parchment paper for printing
  proclamations.
The prince preferred parchment paper for printing
  proclamations.

11

Rainbow Collection

Brian's Burst Blue Balloons

Brian bought blue balloons, but Brian brought the
  balloons back because the balloons burst.
Brian bought blue balloons, but Brian brought the
  balloons back because the balloons burst.
Brian bought blue balloons, but Brian brought the
  balloons back because the balloons burst.

Look! Yellow Laurel Limbs!

"Look, y'all! Yellow laurel limbs!" Lauren yelled.
"Look, y'all! Yellow laurel limbs!" Lauren yelled.
"Look, y'all! Yellow laurel limbs!" Lauren yelled.

Playpens

Pink playpens. Purple playpens.
Pink playpens. Purple playpens.
Pink playpens. Purple playpens.

Big Black Barges

Big black barges bumped bayou bridges.
Big black barges bumped bayou bridges.
Big black barges bumped bayou bridges.

Pretty Plum Pom-poms

Penny planned to purchase pretty plum pom-poms.
Penny planned to purchase pretty plum pom-poms.
Penny planned to purchase pretty plum pom-poms.

Polly's Parents' Party

Polly's parents' party is in the pretty pink parlor.
Polly's parents' party is in the pretty pink parlor.
Polly's parents' party is in the pretty pink parlor.

The Brown Bark Bulged

The brown bark bulged on the bent branch.
The brown bark bulged on the bent branch.
The brown bark bulged on the bent branch.

Red Wood or White Wood?

Was the wood where Woody was red
wood or white wood?
    Was the wood where Woody was red
    wood or white wood?
        Was the wood where Woody was
        red wood or white wood?

The Bowlers' Bowling Balls

The bowlers bought bluish black bowling balls.
The bowlers bought bluish black bowling balls.
The bowlers bought bluish black bowling balls.

Simple Silver Thimbles

Sybil's thimbles are simple silver thimbles.
Sybil's thimbles are simple silver thimbles.
Sybil's thimbles are simple silver thimbles.

12

Feeding Frenzy

Steve and the Steaming Beets

Steve eats steamed beets. Some beets Steve eats leave stains on Steve's sleeves. It seems silly, but Steve still seems to savor the beets he steams.

Sweet, Sticky Syrup Story

The sweet, sticky syrup that stained the sergeant's starched shirt was the same syrup that stained the surgeon's shirt.

Tortilla vs. Fajita

It's neater to eat a tortilla, but it's sweeter to eat a fajita.

It's neater to eat a tortilla, but it's sweeter to eat a fajita.

It's neater to eat a tortilla, but it's sweeter to eat a fajita.

Stacey Street

Stacey Street tried the tasty treat.
Stacey Street tried the tasty treat.
Stacey Street tried the tasty treat.

Crushed Creamed Corn

Quincy crushed a crate of creamed corn.
Quincy crushed a crate of creamed corn.
Quincy crushed a crate of creamed corn.

And Don't Spill It!

Here's a skillet. Fill it with millet and don't spill it.
Here's a skillet. Fill it with millet and don't spill it.
Here's a skillet. Fill it with millet and don't spill it.

Chipped Chopper

Chip couldn't chop chocolate chips 'cause Chip
  chipped his chocolate chip chopper.
Chip couldn't chop chocolate chips 'cause Chip
  chipped his chocolate chip chopper.

Which Dishwasher?

Which dishwasher washed which dish?
Which dishwasher washed which dish?
Which dishwasher washed which dish?

Steak-Thawing Mistake

She thought she thawed the steak, but she thawed the
 stew instead.
She thought she thawed the steak, but she thawed the
 stew instead.
She thought she thawed the steak, but she thawed the
 stew instead.

Ben Baker's Breakfast

Ben Baker had baked beans for breakfast.
Ben Baker had baked beans for breakfast.
Ben Baker had baked beans for breakfast.

Brian Boyle's Breakfast

Brian Boyle brought broiled burgers to breakfast.
Brian Boyle brought broiled burgers to breakfast.
Brian Boyle brought broiled burgers to breakfast.

Super Stew for Stu

The stew is super! Save Stu some.
The stew is super! Save Stu some.
The stew is super! Save Stu some.

Soapy Soup

The soup is soapy. Surely someone
slipped soap in the soup.
    The soup is soapy. Surely someone
slipped soap in the soup.
        The soup is soapy. Surely someone
slipped soap in the soup.

Cooking Corn in Copper Kettles

The cook cooked the corn in copper cooking kettles
'cause copper cooking kettles cook corn quickly.
The cook cooked the corn in copper cooking kettles
'cause copper cooking kettles cook corn quickly.

Papa Porter's Peppered Pickles

Papa Porter purchased a pack of peppered pickles. If
Papa Porter purchased a pack of peppered pickles,
then where's the peppered pickle package Papa
Porter purchased?

Fish Sauce Spoon Loss

I slipped and lost the silver, slotted fish sauce spoon.
I slipped and lost the silver, slotted fish sauce spoon.
I slipped and lost the silver, slotted fish sauce spoon.

Norton Gnaws Noodles

Norton gnaws noodles. Norton is a noodle gnawer.
It's hard to ignore Norton when he's gnawing
noodles. Nobody gnaws noodles like Norton.

Three Free Treats

These three treats are free treats.
These three treats are free treats.
These three treats are free treats.

Saucy Story

I thought he started to sort the sauces, but the sauces
are still unsorted.
I thought he started to sort the sauces, but the sauces
are still unsorted.
I thought he started to sort the sauces, but the sauces
are still unsorted.

13

Class Action

Connor's Laptop

Connor's laptop is apt to topple if Connor keeps it
  atop the counter.
Connor's laptop is apt to topple if Connor keeps it
  atop the counter.
Connor's laptop is apt to topple if Connor keeps it
  atop the counter.

A Proper Place for Pens

Please put your pens, pencils, and posters in the
  proper place.
Please put your pens, pencils, and posters in the
  proper place.
Please put your pens, pencils, and posters in the
  proper place.

Terrible Typing

If the typing is terrible, the typists are
too tired to type.
  If the typing is terrible, the typists are
  too tired to type.
    If the typing is terrible, the typists
    are too tired to type.

Math Master Matt

Matt is a math master. Matt has mastered math.
Matt is a math master. Matt has mastered math.
Matt is a math master. Matt has mastered math.

Heathcliff's Eclipse List

Heathcliff listed each eclipse.
Heathcliff listed each eclipse.
Heathcliff listed each eclipse.

No One Knew

No one knew he knew what he knew.
No one knew he knew what he knew.
No one knew he knew what he knew.

Paddleboat Propulsion

Professor Porter propelled the paddleboat by
  promptly pressing the pedals.
Professor Porter propelled the paddleboat by
  promptly pressing the pedals.
Professor Porter propelled the paddleboat by
  promptly pressing the pedals.

Auditorium Opening

Although Adam offered to open the auditorium early,
  the auditorium didn't open until autumn.
Although Adam offered to open the auditorium early,
  the auditorium didn't open until autumn.

Chauncey Checked the Chalk

Chauncey checked the chalk. Chauncey was a chalk
  checker.
Chauncey checked the chalk. Chauncey was a chalk
  checker.
Chauncey checked the chalk. Chauncey was a chalk
  checker.

School's Rule

The school's rule was that the school fool had to sit
  on the fool stool.
The school's rule was that the school fool had to sit
  on the fool stool.
The school's rule was that the school fool had to sit
  on the fool stool.

Brooke Brought Both Books

Brooke brought both books.
Brooke brought both books.
Brooke brought both books.

14

Varsity Team Twisters

When Juan Runs

When Juan runs, Juan won't rest.
When Juan runs, Juan won't rest.
When Juan runs, Juan won't rest.

Shortstop

The shortstop stopped short.
The shortstop stopped short.
The shortstop stopped short.

The Coach and the Catcher

The coach was concerned that the catcher couldn't catch the curve. The curve came and the catcher caught it. "The catcher caught the curve! Congratulations!"

Watch the Runners Run By?

Want to watch the runners run by? One by one they run.
Want to watch the runners run by? One by one they run.
Want to watch the runners run by? One by one they run.

Cheerleaders Lead Cheers

Cheerleaders lead cheers. The cheers the cheerleaders lead lead the cheerers to cheer loudly.
Cheerleaders lead cheers. The cheers the cheerleaders lead lead the cheerers to cheer loudly.

Better Batters Bat Boldly

The better batters in baseball bat boldly.
The better batters in baseball bat boldly.
The better batters in baseball bat boldly.

15

Home Improvement

Brit Builds Brick Building

Brit is building a brick building.
Brit is building a brick building.
Brit is building a brick building.

Florence Fixed the Faucets

Florence fixed the faulty faucets for us.
Florence fixed the faulty faucets for us.
Florence fixed the faulty faucets for us.

Hey, Hannah!

Hand me the hammer, Hannah.
Hand me the hammer, Hannah.
Hand me the hammer, Hannah.

Hollow-handled Hooks Helpful?

How will hollow-handled hooks help?
How will hollow-handled hooks help?
How will hollow-handled hooks help?

Stella Sawed

Stella sawed a short stick.
Stella sawed a short stick.
Stella sawed a short stick.

Stan Thanked Sam

Stan thanked Sam for sanding the stand.
Stan thanked Sam for sanding the stand.
Stan thanked Sam for sanding the stand.

Patty Painted Plaid Patterns

Patty painted plaid patterns.
Patty painted plaid patterns.
Patty painted plaid patterns.

Stinky Sink

The sink stinks. It's a stinky sink.
The sink stinks. It's a stinky sink.
The sink stinks. It's a stinky sink.

Where's the Wire Rope?

Where's the wire rope?
Where's the wire rope?
Where's the wire rope?

Ladder Lending

When Noel wouldn't loan Euell a yellow ladder, Euell yelled.

When Noel wouldn't loan Euell a yellow ladder, Euell yelled.

When Noel wouldn't loan Euell a yellow ladder, Euell yelled.

Hedda's Head

Hedda hit her hard hat hard. However, her head hardly hurt.

Hedda hit her hard hat hard. However, her head hardly hurt.

Hedda hit her hard hat hard. However, her head hardly hurt.

16

Alphabet Soup

Aches and Achers

Avril's ears ache and Arvel's ankles ache.
Avril's ears ache and Arvel's ankles ache.
Avril's ears ache and Arvel's ankles ache.

Blank Blackboards

Blaine brought the blackboards. The blackboards
  Blaine bought were blank.
Blaine brought the blackboards. The blackboards
  Blaine bought were blank.
Blaine brought the blackboards. The blackboards
  Blaine bought were blank.

Carter's Clean Coat

Carter's clean coat is in the cluttered coat closet.
Carter's clean coat is in the cluttered coat closet.
Carter's clean coat is in the cluttered coat closet.

Contagious Kitty?

Could a kid catch a cold from a kitty cat
that caught a cold?
  Could a kid catch a cold from a kitty
  cat that caught a cold?
    Could a kid catch a cold from a
    kitty cat that caught a cold?

Ditch Diggers Do

Ditch diggers dig ditches. That's what ditch diggers do.
Ditch diggers dig ditches. That's what ditch diggers do.
Ditch diggers dig ditches. That's what ditch diggers do.

Emma's Mama

Emma's mama and Emma's mawmaw made Emma a
muumuu.
Emma's mama and Emma's mawmaw made Emma a
muumuu.
Emma's mama and Emma's mawmaw made Emma a
muumuu.

Frances Fancies

Frances fancies frilly flowers.
Frances fancies frilly flowers.
Frances fancies frilly flowers.

Hidden High Heels

Heidi had to hide her high heels.
Heidi had to hide her high heels.
Heidi had to hide her high heels.

Ken Can't

Kenny the canner can't can a can of corn, can he?
Kenny the canner can't can a can of corn, can he?
Kenny the canner can't can a can of corn, can he?

Let's Look for Lester's Lost List

Lester said he lost the list, but I think Lester left the list in the loft.

Lester said he lost the list, but I think Lester left the list in the loft.

Lester said he lost the list, but I think Lester left the list in the loft.

Lou's Loops

Lou's loops are loose loops.
Lou's loops are loose loops.
Lou's loops are loose loops.

Messy Mustard Making

Making mustard is messy, and mustard mixers are
master mess makers.

Making mustard is messy, and mustard mixers are
master mess makers.

Making mustard is messy, and mustard mixers are
master mess makers.

Noel's Non-News

Noel knows no news about the noodles Newt needs.
Noel knows no news about the noodles Newt needs.
Noel knows no news about the noodles Newt needs.

Paula Perched a Parrot

Paula perched her parrot on the pretty plastic plant.
Paula perched her parrot on the pretty plastic plant.
Paula perched her parrot on the pretty plastic plant.

Sue's Shoes

Sue's shoes are soiled.
Sue's shoes are soiled.
Sue's shoes are soiled.

Tall Troll Throws Toad

Did the tall troll throw the toad through
the toll tunnel?
Did the tall troll throw the toad
through the toll tunnel?
Did the tall troll throw the toad
through the toll tunnel?

Warm Armor Mystery Solved

Warren's armor was warm because Warren wore an
armor-warmer.
Warren's armor was warm because Warren wore an
armor-warmer.
Warren's armor was warm because Warren wore an
armor-warmer.

eddy Bye Bye

The Clock

The clock ticked. The clock tocked. The clock tick-tocked.

The clock ticked. The clock tocked. The clock tick-tocked.

The clock ticked. The clock tocked. The clock tick-tocked.

Somber Sweeper

The somber sweeper swept the streets while
  slumbering sleepers snored.
The somber sweeper swept the streets while
  slumbering sleepers snored.
The somber sweeper swept the streets while
  slumbering sleepers snored.

Puppy Pillow

Priscilla's sister plumped Patricia's
puppy's puppy pillow.
    Priscilla's sister plumped Patricia's
    puppy's puppy pillow.
        Priscilla's sister plumped Patricia's
        puppy's puppy pillow.

Shhh! Sleeping Sheep!

See the sheep sleep? They are sleepy sheep.
See the sheep sleep? They are sleepy sheep.
See the sheep sleep? They are sleepy sheep.

Soft Silky Slippers

Sylvia saw some soft silky slippers.
Sylvia saw some soft silky slippers.
Sylvia saw some soft silky slippers.

Sleepy Dee

Dee is sleeping deeply. Dee is a deep sleeper. The
  deeper Dee sleeps, the sleepier Dee seems.
Dee is sleeping deeply. Dee is a deep sleeper. The
  deeper Dee sleeps, the sleepier Dee seems.

Shutter Diplomacy

Shannon shut some shutters, but she didn't shut other
  shutters. The sun will surely shine through the
  shutters Shannon didn't shut.

A Dream for Danielle

Danielle dreams that dragons dance on
Dustin's drip-dried drapes.
  Danielle dreams that dragons dance
  on Dustin's drip-dried drapes.
    Danielle dreams that dragons dance
    on Dustin's drip-dried drapes.

Loose Luke

Let's let Luke loose.
Let's let Luke loose.
Let's let Luke loose.

Tex's Excellent Exit

Although it took extra effort for Tex to exit, Tex
  exited excellently.
Although it took extra effort for Tex to exit, Tex
  exited excellently.
Although it took extra effort for Tex to exit, Tex
  exited excellently.

ndex